VR ON THE JOB
**Understanding Virtual
and Augmented Reality**

USING VR IN ENGINEERING

Sara Chuirazzi

Cavendish
Square

New York

Published in 2020 by Cavendish Square Publishing, LLC
243 5th Avenue, Suite 136, New York, NY 10016

Website: cavendishsq.com

This publication represents the opinions and views of the author based on his or her personal
experience, knowledge, and research. The information in this book serves as a general
guide only. The author and publisher have used their best efforts in preparing this book and
disclaim liability rising directly or indirectly from the use and application of this book.

All websites were available and accurate when this book was sent to press.

Library of Congress Cataloging-in-Publication Data

Names: Chuirazzi, Sara, author.
Title: Using VR in engineering / Sara Chuirazzi.
Description: First edition. | New York : Cavendish Square, 2020. | Series: VR on the job : understanding
virtual and augmented reality | Audience: Grades 7-12. | Includes bibliographical references and index.
Identifiers: LCCN 2018058462 (print) | LCCN 2018061638 (ebook) |
ISBN 9781502645654 (ebook) | ISBN 9781502645647 (library bound) | ISBN 9781502645630 (pbk.)
Subjects: LCSH: Virtual reality in engineering--Vocational guidance--Juvenile literature. |
Augmented reality--Vocational guidance--Juvenile literature.
Classification: LCC QA76.9.C65 (ebook) | LCC QA76.9.C65 C485 2020 (print) |
DDC 006.8--dc23
LC record available at https://lccn.loc.gov/2018058462

Editorial Director: David McNamara
Editor: Chet'la Sebree
Copy Editor: Nathan Heidelberger
Associate Art Director: Alan Sliwinski
Designer: Christina Shults
Production Coordinator: Karol Szymczuk
Photo Research: J8 Media

The photographs in this book are used by permission and through the courtesy of:
Cover Georgejmclittle/Shutterstock.com, background (and used throughout the book) Click
Bestsellers/Shutterstock.com; p. 4 Faiz Zaki/Shutterstock.com; p. 8 Boston Globe/Getty Images; p.
10 picture alliance/Getty Images; p. 12 NASA/Wikimedia Commons/File:Evelyn Miralles at NASA.
jpg/CC0; p. 15 flowgraph/Shutterstock.com; p. 18 Cultura Creative(RF)/Alamy Stock Photo; p.
20 Fernando Blanco Calzada/Shutterstock.com; p. 24 Bodnar Taras/Shutterstock.com; p. 27 AFP/
Getty Images; pp. 28-29 gorodenkoff/iStock/Getty Images; p. 30 SpeedKingz/Shutterstock.com;
p. 34 iinspiration/Shutterstock.com; p. 36 adventtr/iStock/Getty Images; p. 39 jeffbergen/E+/
Getty Images; p. 41 Kzenon/Shutterstock.com; pp. 46, 51 Monkey Business Images/Shutterstock.
com; pp. 52-53 fstop123/E+/Getty Images; pp. 54, 62 ©AP Images; p. 56 wavebreakmedia/
Shutterstock.com; p. 60 Dmitri Ma/Shutterstock.com; pp. 64-65 Uladzik Kryhin/Shutterstock.com;
p. 67 Claus Lunau/Science Photo Library/Getty Images; p. 68 PeopleImages/E+/Getty Images.

Printed in the United States of America

CONTENTS

1 A NEW REALITY

The use of virtual and augmented reality in different job markets has been steadily growing since the 1980s. However, virtual and augmented reality technology is still considered relatively new. That means that many of the engineering-related careers in the field involve developing the technology to support virtual and augmented reality. This includes both the software, meaning programs and operating systems used by computers, and the hardware, meaning physical equipment like headsets.

Opposite: Standard virtual reality (VR) headsets are worn like goggles over a user's eyes. They aim to block out external light and distractions so that users can be fully immersed in a digital landscape.

ENGINEERS ON THE FOREFRONT

Engineers are the leaders in this exciting new field. They are responsible for the behind-the-scenes work that makes virtual and augmented reality possible. The technology that they create is used for cars, railroads, shipbuilding, aerospace design, and general construction. Even though the technology is used widely, engineers have to make sure that it can fulfill very specific needs. Their goal is to make the technology as easy and efficient to use as possible.

Before beginning to understand how these different technologies affect the specific jobs listed above, it's important to understand the differences between virtual reality (VR) and augmented reality (AR), as well the history of these technologies.

A BRIEF HISTORY

Jaron Lanier created the term "virtual reality" in 1987. He was a computer scientist and artist. Virtual reality is the use of a computer to stimulate a user's senses. These stimulated senses allow a person to interact with three-dimensional (3D) images or other sensory stimuli, or things that cause a reaction. VR applications place users in computer-generated environments that present an alternate reality.

VR programs often use interactive devices. These devices are worn as goggles, headsets, gloves, or bodysuits. These components send and receive information to and from the user and the technology. For instance, gloves or bodysuits send information to the technology about the ways in which the user is moving his or her body. The technology can send similar information. For example, as the technology receives information about the user's movements, the user can see his or her movements on the screen. Similarly, the gloves can send signals to users' hands so that they feel like they're touching things that they see themselves touching in the digital environment.

Early on, VR development was funded by the federal government. Organizations such as the Department of Defense, the National Science Foundation, and the National Aeronautics and Space Administration (NASA) were some of the earliest supporters. These organizations were eager to develop the technology. It created connections between academia, the military, and the workforce. For instance, VR simulators imitating flight were used to train military pilots.

Another important figure in VR development was Joseph Carl Robnett Licklider. He was a professor at the Massachusetts Institute of Technology (MIT). He founded the Information Processing Techniques Office (IPTO) in 1964.

IPTO was part of a larger federal agency called the Defense Advanced Research Projects Agency (DARPA). DARPA develops emerging, or newer, technology for the military. It was created in February 1958 in response to the Soviet Union, present-day Russia, launching its first satellite in October 1957. In fact, according to DARPA's history, the US government created it to "keep ... technological superiority in the hands of the United States."

Professor Joseph Carl Robnett Licklider (*left*), of the Massachusetts Institute of Technology (MIT), works with his student Jeff Harris (*right*). Licklider founded the Information Processing Techniques Office (IPTO) in 1964.

Within DARPA, IPTO funded projects that focused on interactions between humans and computers. Licklider hoped that one day the two would interact seamlessly. In 2010, IPTO became DAPRA's Information Innovation Office.

Engineer and computer scientist Ivan Sutherland also played a key role at DARPA. After receiving his doctorate from MIT, he served in the US Army as an electrical engineer. This type of engineer has a specific knowledge related to the operations of electrical systems. Sutherland served in the National Security Agency (NSA) and then DARPA. While an engineer for DARPA, he started working on projects related to artificial intelligence, when computers perform tasks associated with living beings. Later, Sutherland was also the head of the computer graphics department at the University of Utah. This department is one of DARPA's most highly regarded research centers.

During his time as a graduate student at MIT, however, he created Sketchpad. It was the first interactive computer graphics program. Sketchpad allowed users to draw and visualize designs. It quickly became a foundational building block in the creation and development of virtual reality.

TWO TYPES OF REALITY

Virtual reality is a fully immersive experience that works to remove distractions from the outside world. Augmented reality, however, adds digital elements to a user's real-

Italian rowers wore smart glasses to help them train for the 2016 Summer Olympics in Rio de Janeiro.

life field of vision. In this way, it augments, or adds to, a person's existing reality.

Google Cardboard is an example of virtual reality. This simple, affordable cardboard box allows users to place their phone inside, turn on one of many apps, and hold it up to their eyes. This allows users to experience situations and places that they may otherwise never experience. Some even say that it provides a somewhat "out-of-body" experience. Someone looking through Google Cardboard might see a campfire scene complete with a tent, trees, and maybe even perfectly toasted s'mores. By using a mobile phone, users have the ability to add sound to the experience, such as the crackling of a fire, crickets chirping, and the wind moving through trees. When using Google Cardboard, an entirely new field of vision is presented through the phone and the headset.

Meanwhile, examples of augmented reality include Snapchat filters and *Pokémon Go*. The Snapchat filters impose virtual elements over photos. *Pokémon Go* places characters in a user's visual world accessed through the phone's camera. Users can imagine that Pokémon characters are living in the same world as them as users capture them throughout their neighborhoods.

Another example of AR technology is smart glasses. Smart glasses are computer-operated glasses that project information onto a user's field of vision. For instance, bike riders can use the technology to track their speed and heart rate. They can also use these glasses to navigate without

ANOTHER HIDDEN FIGURE

Like the African American women involved in the 1960s space race made famous by Margot Lee Shetterly's *Hidden Figures*, Evelyn Miralles is a woman making waves at NASA today. Miralles, a computer engineer, specializes in VR innovation at NASA's Johnson Space Center in Houston, Texas.

She started at the government agency in the early 1990s, designing graphics software and creating tools for space flight training. Thanks to her unique knowledge and expertise, most space missions since

Evelyn Miralles, a principal engineer and innovator at NASA's Virtual Reality Laboratory (VRLab), started working on space missions in 1992.

1992 have not happened without her involvement. In fact, since the turn of the century, Miralles has worked on most space shuttle and International Space Station missions. Her innovative technologies have helped prepare astronauts for experiences unique to outer space.

Although she may not be a household name, Miralles has contributed groundbreaking work to the engineering field. One of her greatest professional achievements is Dynamic Onboard Ubiquitous Graphics (DOUG), a project for which she was one of the lead developers. It was initially used to train astronauts to repair the Hubble Space Telescope. It has also been used to simulate extravehicular activity (EVA), also known as spacewalking, and to teach crewmembers how to navigate certain tasks required of their missions.

Miralles is the principal engineer and innovator at NASA's Virtual Reality Laboratory (VRLab). There she leads a team developing programs for a mission to Mars.

In addition to her distinction in the VR community, Miralles is also dedicated to giving back. She encourages students, particularly young women, to develop an interest in science, technology, engineering, and mathematics (STEM). Not only is she a pioneer as one of the few women in a male-dominated field, but she is one of the first Latinx women to make a name for herself in VR. In 2016, she was recognized as one of the British Broadcasting Corporation's 100 Inspirational Women in the World.

having to disrupt their ride to look at a watch or a screen mounted on their handlebars.

Although they are separate technologies, VR and AR are often discussed in the same circles. A new industry term for the combined VR/AR field is "extended reality," often referred to as XR.

A THIRD PLAYER, PERHAPS: MIXED REALITY

In addition to virtual and augmented reality, "mixed reality" is another term used in the XR field. In fact, there is some confusion surrounding the term. Sometimes mixed reality is characterized as anything that falls between the real world and virtual reality, which includes augmented reality. Other times, people define mixed reality as its own division of XR, aside from augmented reality.

Either way, mixed reality falls between the two opposite ends of the "virtuality continuum." This term was created in 1994 by Paul Milgram and Fumio Kishino to describe the span between virtual and physical realities. Today, this continuum is commonly referred to as the "mixed reality spectrum." A spectrum depicts two extreme opposites and all that falls between them. On the mixed reality spectrum, humans are situated at the far left. This space represents physical reality and the real world, without any digital intervention. On the right-hand side is digital reality, or virtual reality. Experiences that remove outside distractions and take over your view to present a digital world are virtual reality.

This Microsoft HoloLens headset replaces this student's physical world with an immersive, 3D digital experience of a particular car model.

Augmented and mixed realities, whether defined as the same or separate entities, fall in the middle of this spectrum. Mixed reality in its ideal form is the combination of computer processing (the technology being used), human input (people interacting with the technology), and environmental input (physical boundaries, sounds, lighting, location, etc.).

Mixed reality, like augmented reality, attempts to break down the barriers between physical and digital worlds. Unlike augmented reality, which overlays graphics or videos onto your physical world, mixed reality can start in either the physical or virtual world. For instance, for mixed reality environments set in the real world, people can interact with digital objects much in the same way they can with augmented reality.

However, mixed reality isn't limited to that experience. It also includes experiences set, technically, in virtual reality. For mixed reality environments that begin in the virtual world, however, the virtual world is constructed out of the real one. Consider this: You're in your bedroom. You slip on a mixed reality headset, and the virtual world is identical to your bedroom. Although you are fully immersed, you are experiencing your real world as you move through it. The virtual images overlap with the real ones. Typically, virtual reality environments are constructed to transport you into an entirely new environment. With mixed reality headsets, a person's environment is captured, mapped, and constructed in a digital space.

Holographic devices are examples of this type of technology. They are characterized by the ability to place digital elements into a user's reality. The Microsoft HoloLens is a headset that is considered a holographic device. HoloLens technology allows engineers to visualize full-scale 3D models, design spaces, and connect with other designers in real time in their own environments. For instance, an engineer in New York City can view, through the HoloLens, an engineer in San Francisco's current work environment. This technology makes it easier for teams to collaborate and increases prototyping, or modeling, speed.

Although it can be difficult to decide which term to use for which technology, it's important to remember that they are all XR technologies.

SO, WHAT ABOUT ENGINEERS?

Engineers are incredibly important to the VR/AR field. They are the people responding to the needs of users in this quickly growing area. Engineers are also responsible for brainstorming new ways to use the technology. They must focus on making existing technology as useful as possible, while also looking ahead for other ways that it might be able to serve people across different careers. The interesting thing about engineers in this field is that they are deeply involved in every stage of virtual and augmented reality development. Their voices shape the technology and how it's used.

2 THE PRACTICAL VALUE OF EXTENDED REALITY

Engineers play a very important role in the existence of virtual and augmented reality. They create, program, and adapt software and hardware that everyone else uses. Although virtual and augmented reality have mainly been used by gaming companies and in the military, their usage has continued to grow and expand, largely for practical reasons.

COMPUTER-AIDED ENGINEERING

An important intersection of engineering and virtual and augmented reality is computer-aided engineering (CAE). CAE is the combination of design and manufacturing into a system that computers can manage and control. Specifically, CAE is a combination

Opposite: Engineers use computer-aided engineering (CAE) in car production factories. CAE technology allows them to draw, develop, and revise realistic models that are used to manufacture cars.

A designer works on a computer-aided design (CAD) blueprint. CAD blueprints are used to plan and design products by using computer graphics.

of computer-aided design (CAD) and computer-aided manufacturing (CAM). For that reason, sometimes CAE is referred to as CAD/CAM.

Computer-aided design refers to the use of computers to plan products, especially using computer graphics. A CAD system usually consists of a computer with video monitors and interactive devices (such as headsets).

Computer-aided manufacturing is the use of computers that have been specially programmed to operate machinery without human intervention. CAM systems rely on machines that are similar to programmable robots. This means that they can carry out a task automatically after the initial programming.

CAE, the combination of these two technologies, allows engineers to create realistic, 3D computer models. It also allows them to more easily envision and test how products will stand up to real-world conditions. Engineers use CAE systems to draw, develop, and revise designs. These designs are then turned into step-by-step instructions that machines are able to use to manufacture objects.

Virtual and augmented reality programs allow engineers to map out how a machine will perform a task. They can also be useful in showing engineers where robots might get stuck. The technology can also help engineers identify how something may need to be programmed differently because of environmental factors. For example, if a machine is programmed to insert a special piece into a computer, engineers can determine the precise placement depending on the environment. They can even delay the time in between each placement using CAD sketches.

As an example, let's take a look at how this technology is used in the shipbuilding field. Engineers can use VR/AR headsets or smart glasses to view their ship designs as 3D models. This allows them to virtually examine and test the structure of the ships. They can then make changes where necessary. Using a CAE system reduces the time commitment that building physical models involves. It also increases productivity by making it easier to make changes during the process of designing and building. Similar systems are used in designing cars, railroads, and major architectural projects, such as bridges or skyscrapers.

AEROSPACE DESIGN AND OPERATION

One of the first industries that virtual and augmented reality was developed for was the aerospace field. Aerospace refers to airplane and space flights. CAE technology is used widely by Embraer, a Brazilian aerospace company that produces commercial, military, executive, and agricultural aircrafts. The company's Virtual Reality Center was established in February 2000 in Brazil. The center is equipped with a computer that allows engineers to visualize 3D models of the aircrafts. This is an example of how VR/AR is used at the planning and prototype phases of aircraft design. A prototype is the initial model of something, from which more models can be built.

As with shipbuilding, a benefit of using this technology to create aircraft models is that engineers don't have to invest the time and money that would otherwise be required to design and build prototypes. In addition to visualizing the structure of aircrafts, engineers can also play around with the way a plane looks. For example, they can run tests to see where the logo is most visible. From a safety standpoint, they can also experiment with where the lights are most useful and how models withstand windspeeds.

CAVE AUTOMATIC VIRTUAL ENVIRONMENTS

Cave automatic virtual environments (also referred to as CAVE technology) are room-sized visualization systems that provide users with an immersive virtual reality experience. CAVE technology was designed at the University of Indiana in the late 1970s. The cube-like space is designed to project images onto the walls from floor to ceiling, like a cave. CAVE technology can also allow multiple users to enjoy the same virtual environment simultaneously.

Much like with a virtual reality center, engineers can use CAVE technology to interact with virtual prototypes. Oftentimes headsets or touch-sensitive gloves are used to visualize and touch a digital version of the product. These interactive devices display 3D images created by computers. Another key part of the technology is how humans interact with it. Instead of using a joystick or controller, like you might with a video game console, users can use their hands to pull, twist, and grip. This ability to interact with the technology is referred to as haptics. These haptics offer real-life experiences with CAVE technology.

Ford has a 3D cave automatic virtual environment to design and test new cars digitally. This reduces costs associated with building physical prototypes. Inside the CAVE is a model of a car interior. Remote controls are used to adjust the virtual steering wheel and rearview mirrors. Users can even open virtual glove compartments. All of these actions are done by clicking and holding buttons on

A car simulator can be used for entertainment but also allows engineers to test out the functionality and safety of vehicles.

the remote controls. With CAVE technology, engineers can compare how different designs affect a driver's experience.

General Motors (GM) also uses CAVE technology. In addition to testing out functionality, or quality of use, of vehicles, safety can be evaluated. Engineers can use this technology to simulate crashes to determine how cars might react to specific crash conditions.

THE CHANGING LANDSCAPE OF ENGINEERING

XR technologies have changed almost all jobs in the engineering field. CAD technology has replaced the need to build physical models of products. That means that technology has replaced some of the manual labor jobs in the field. Many engineers, however, have learned to adapt and use VR and AR in their jobs. Instead of investing time and energy working on physical models and multiple paper drafts, engineers might now spend that time creating CAD sketches, which are easier to edit, and modeling with CAVE software. Additionally, there is more time for these engineers to create even newer models or pursue new ideas. This additional time allows for more innovation and experimentation in the field.

Training VR/AR Engineers

The engineering field has experienced many changes over the past thirty years. Because of this, training is an important factor in the success of individual engineers and the field as a whole.

A company called Honeywell worked with Microsoft to create a set of training programs. They're called "Connected Plant Skills Insight Immersive Competency" programs and are stored in a cloud network. A cloud network is a communication system that can be accessed by people all over the world. The Honeywell programs offer on-the-job

DIGITAL RESPONSIBILITY AND DRAWBACKS OF VR/AR

In such a fast-moving industry, it's important to take time to consider how technology is changing our everyday world. Like with most things, there are pros and cons, or positive and negative factors, that come with the development and usage of extended reality. In regards to mental health, researchers have noted that VR and AR can lead to decreased attention spans. Similarly, they can lead to a sense of isolation and underdeveloped social skills, as users can spend large stretches of time alone with the technology.

Because the software is so immersive, it's possible that users get scared or feel uneasy, especially when playing video games. For example, if the VR scene has them walking on a plank over a canyon or experiencing a high-speed car chase, they might feel anxious or motion sick. Headaches and eye strain are also side effects of using technology.

Studies have shown that XR in general can influence the way a person behaves and thinks even after using the technology. Designers must weigh the pros and cons of creating experiences that have the ability to affect users long after they take their headsets off. Software developers have a responsibility to consider ethics, or the principles of right and wrong behavior, when designing and testing new technology. This means making design decisions that serve helpful, productive purposes with awareness of their potentially harmful impact. This concept is often referred to as digital responsibility.

This woman's bodysuit captures her movements and transmits information between her and the computer.

training for engineers who need to learn to incorporate new VR and AR technologies into their daily processes.

Experiential learning is the process of learning by doing. Usually, it is followed by discussing potential outcomes or solutions to problems. Honeywell offers these types of learning opportunities for engineers working in industrial and manufacturing plants or factories. There are

Virtual reality headsets allow users to interact with data and images that can be created and manipulated.

also programs for engineers working in the field.

One of the training programs uses Microsoft's HoloLens, Windows Mixed Reality, and Honeywell's C300 controller. The controller is a piece of hardware that has the ability to model various learning scenarios. The program can be used to model what happens when a machine fails to do what it's designed to do. This tests users on their problem-solving skills. The trainer can then walk the users through possible solutions, and the experience becomes more collaborative and realistic.

3 VR/AR JOBS IN ENGINEERING

Engineering as a whole consists of many different, smaller areas of focus. These include mechanical, chemical, electrical, civil, and software engineering, among many others. This variety of focuses means that there are plenty of on-the-ground engineering jobs beyond software development. For instance, these jobs exist in design and maritime, or shipbuilding, fields. There are also careers available outside of the traditional designing and building engineering jobs. Many people with engineering backgrounds work in jobs related to education and training, sales, marketing, consulting, and public relations. VR and AR have also spread into health care. With this great diversity of jobs, it can be difficult to know where to even begin searching

Opposite: In addition to learning about virtual and augmented reality technologies, engineers interested in extended reality need to have a good understanding of how to design and build.

for jobs related to extended reality. In this chapter, we'll take a look at a few diverse jobs in the engineering field.

CAREERS IN THE FIELD

The Bureau of Labor Statistics (BLS) is a federal agency. It is responsible for measuring labor market activity, work conditions, and the changing prices of goods and services in the United States. The BLS reports that employment in the computer and informational technology job sector is expected to grow 13 percent between 2016 and 2026. This is faster than the average rate of growth for all occupations. This growth is expected to create about 557,100 new jobs in the field. This increase in jobs will increase the demand for people with STEM (science, technology, engineering, and mathematics) degrees and experience.

SOFTWARE ENGINEER

Level:	Entry-level
Years of Experience Required:	Zero
Education Needed:	Bachelor's degree in computer science, information technology, engineering, mathematics, or a related field
Skills Needed:	Strong interpersonal, problem-solving, and computer programming skills

A software engineer, often called a "junior engineer," is one of the most common entry-level jobs. This job provides people with the opportunity to grow and progress in their careers. Most software engineering jobs require you to have a degree in a related field. It is also often a plus to have had exposure to computer-programming languages such as JavaScript, which is a computer language used to create interactive websites. Similarly, it is good to have HTML, or hypertext markup language, experience. The HTML coding language is used to build basic websites.

Being a software engineer involves working with a team of people at various skill levels to develop, test, implement, and maintain computer applications and programs. For this reason, it is incredibly important for potential software engineers to be able to effectively collaborate and work together on a team.

Software engineers also work to improve the performance of existing software and to update it to respond to changes in the technology or market. Engineers designing any kind of software should carefully consider how users will interact with it. They should aim to maximize functionality. Maximizing functionality can involve fixing problems and developing new strategies. For that reason, it's important for people interested in this type of career to have excellent problem-solving skills.

A common job for software engineers is designing apps. Apps are specialized programs developed to execute a specific function. For instance, Google Maps is an application specifically designed to help people figure

```
<!DOCTYPE html>
<html xmlns="http://www.w3.org/1999/xhtml">
<head>
    <title>Sample HTML Page</title>
        <meta http-equiv="Content-type" content="t
        <meta property="og:type" content="website"
        <meta property="og:url" content="http://ww
        <meta name="robots" content="index, follow
        <meta name="author" content="http://www.so
        <link href="http://www.somedomain.com/" re
        <link href="http://www.somedomain.com/" re
        <script type='text/javascript' src='http:/
        <script type='text/javascript' src='http:/
</head>
<body>
<div class="mainHeader">
```

HTML is a computer programming language used to design and develop
basic web pages and create interactive sites.

out where they are and where they are going. These jobs
are so common these days because of people's increased
reliance on mobile technology. Mobile technology is one of
the top three industries in technology. In the United States,
there will be more than 222,000 software development jobs
created between 2012 and 2022.

INTERACTION/USER EXPERIENCE DESIGNER

Level:	Mid-level
Years of Experience Required:	Three to five years
Education Needed:	Bachelor's degree in design, user experience, human-computer interaction, or a related field
Skills Needed:	Experience in 3D graphics, real-time rendering (creating images that move realistically), and developing or prototyping VR/AR experiences.

Software engineers can move into interaction or user experience design as they progress in their careers. These positions are considered more advanced jobs. Companies like Google and Amazon hire for these types of positions. According to the Interaction Design Association, "Interaction designers strive to create meaningful relationships between people and the products and services that they use from computers to mobile devices to appliances and beyond." In other words, these designers are responsible for best understanding and creating strong and purposeful engagements between users and devices.

Three-dimensional models allow engineers to virtually examine and test the structure of their designs. In some cases, 3D printers are used to create solid objects from these digital designs.

Interaction or user experience (UX) designers' salaries are based on experience levels. Although this job usually requires a bachelor's degree in a related field, sometimes companies will hire people with equivalent experience in the workforce. This experience usually has to include designing visual and interactive models, creating concepts for new products, managing a variety of projects, and being attentive to how users use the software.

At this level, it's also important to have some general experience using 3D graphics to design virtual and augmented reality experiences. Those skills will be helpful in generating realistic models using computer programs.

SENIOR SYSTEMS ENGINEER

Level:	Mid-level
Years of Experience Required:	Five or more years
Education Needed:	Bachelor's degree in engineering, information systems, computer science, or a related field; at this level, however, a master's degree is often preferred
Skills Needed:	Strong interpersonal skills, background in electronics or communications, and an understanding of both software and hardware

Systems engineering is a branch of engineering that introduces new technology into the development stage of a system. It is an interdisciplinary branch that requires people to assess risk, understand work processes, and streamline processes. The goal of systems engineering is usually to use new technology as quickly as possible.

Systems engineers are usually more common at a senior level and tend to have a background in electronics or communications. This type of job usually requires a bachelor's degree in engineering, information systems, computer science, or a related field, and at least five years of industry experience. At some levels, a master's degree in computer science, computer information systems, or engineering may be required. Companies like General Motors and Qualcomm, a telecommunications company, hire for positions like this.

Senior system engineers in the AR and VR field are responsible for thinking ahead and considering how augmented and virtual reality might be optimized. Optimization means that the technologies perform in the most effective way possible. System engineers should be able to collaborate with both software and hardware teams to design solutions for products that support VR and AR applications. For that reason, strong interpersonal skills are required for this job as well.

Training programs and experiential learning opportunities are keys to success. These opportunities are available for engineers working in multiple industries.

SOURCING MANAGER

Level:	Managerial
Years of Experience Required:	Ten or more years
Education Needed:	Bachelor's degree in engineering, information systems, computer science, or a related field; at this level, however, a master's degree is often preferred
Skills Needed:	Management experience and an understanding of the technologies

A sourcing manager is a manager-level job. It tends to be more communications- and education-focused than some of the more technical careers mentioned throughout this book. That being said, sourcing managers are critical to success in the XR field. They are responsible for hiring and training engineers. Companies like Facebook are hiring VR/AR-specific sourcing managers to create new hardware and software products. The goal is to make the products social and immersive.

This position usually requires ten or more years of recruiting experience and at least four years of managing teams of six or more employees. Sourcing managers need to be excellent communicators and multitaskers. Another important part of this job is to partner with hiring managers in an effort to develop a detailed profile

Jobs in engineering often require collaborating with others. Having strong interpersonal and communications skills are an important part of being successful in the field.

USING EXTENDED REALITY IN OUR DAILY LIVES

Engineers are responsible for designing virtual and augmented reality programs for use in military, gaming, and medical fields. They also use the technology in their own day-to-day jobs. IrisVR is a company that creates technology that easily fits into the everyday engineering workflow. This technology is specifically helpful to civil engineers, who often focus on construction and architecture. With special programs designed to aid architecture and construction, the software helps to create 3D experiences that reduce time, money, and materials spent building prototypes.

IrisVR's more intensive Prospect and mobile-compatible Scope software also help to streamline projects. Both programs allow teams to directly input specific and useful feedback. The common language provided by the 3D models in these programs increases safety and reduces on-site risks. The sort of daily usefulness of these technologies, however, extends beyond the engineering field.

Even before *Pokémon Go*, ordinary people were using XR apps. Although no longer in use, CityViewAR was one of the early apps that allowed people to use AR. In September 2010, Christchurch, New Zealand, was hit by multiple large-scale earthquakes. They damaged much of the city. While Christchurch was under reconstruction, people had trouble navigating without familiar landmarks. It was disorienting. From that frustration, CityViewAR was born.

This mobile AR application allowed people to look through their phones and see the city as it was before the earthquake. People were able to walk around their city "seeing" life-sized 3D models of buildings through their smartphones. The images were created using photos and building histories made available by organizations throughout the city. CityViewAR pulled from GPS and compass sensors in phones to overlay virtual information on live video of the real world.

of candidates. Sourcing managers also need to be able to use data to identify trends in the field. This allows them to develop creative recruitment strategies and provide decision-makers with insights.

Sourcing managers are also responsible for onboarding employees. This means that it's the sourcing manager's responsibility to make sure that new employees are properly trained and oriented to the company. Beyond that, these managers also need to make sure that current employees are reaching career milestones that serve the company as a whole.

DIRECTOR OF VENTURE PROGRAMS OR CORPORATE INNOVATIONS

Level:	Senior
Average Salary Range:	Varies
Years of Experience Required:	Seven or more years
Education Needed:	A master's degree is often preferred
Skills Needed:	Experience managing programs in the tech industry, developing products, team building, and raising capital; additionally, strong interpersonal, written, and verbal communication skills

A director of venture programs or corporate innovations is a senior-level position. These jobs can exist within universities or in corporate America. Having a master's degree makes candidates more competitive for this type of position. Additionally, people at this level usually have at least seven years of progressive experience, or experiences within increasing responsibilities. Experience in the tech industry—specifically with product development, management, business development, and team building— is often helpful.

It's also important for these individuals to have experience raising capital, or money, for the company or university center for which they work. Positions like these are especially important to start-ups focused on virtual and augmented reality. These businesses are usually driven by entrepreneurs. An entrepreneur is a person who takes the initiative to start and manage a new business, usually taking on sizeable risk in the process. A director of venture programs will help gather the funds needed for VR and AR projects. Similarly, a director of corporate innovations will help attract partners, investors, and funders for projects. They will also build strong relationships and partnerships with major and start-up tech companies, foundations, and corporations.

In addition to more practical experience in the field, venture program and corporate innovations directors should be able to clearly communicate with entrepreneurs and corporate intrapreneurs. An intrapreneur is an employee who creates new products, services, and systems with a company's support. Directors at this level support entrepreneurs and intrapreneurs at all stages of their business development.

For these reasons, these jobs require exceptional communication skills, organizational skills, and the ability to self-manage. Additionally, it is important for a person pursuing a director role to be able to embrace uncertainty and problem-solve when needed.

EXPANDING HORIZONS

These are just a few of the many career options available to students interested in extended reality and engineering. One of the most exciting parts of this industry is that it's new. While that means that there are still a lot of questions about it, it also means that the possibilities are endless.

Is there a job that sounds interesting to you but isn't one that you've necessarily heard of? That doesn't mean that it's not important or that it can't exist one day. Asking questions and knocking on doors is an important part of the work that engineers in this industry do. They look beyond what already is to envision what might be possible.

4 CAREER PREP

igh school is a great time to look into relevant internships, summer jobs, and camps. These opportunities will help you to further explore your interests in both engineering and extended reality careers. A good place to start is to take a look at your school's course catalog. Plan on taking as many math and computer science courses as possible because careers with a focus on technology require those skills.

COURSEWORK

STEM courses in general are helpful for a career in both VR/AR and engineering. A good amount of the work that computer engineers do requires understanding computers, which are run by numbers. For that reason,

Opposite: Internships and summer jobs provide opportunities to further explore careers in engineering and extended reality, as well as chances to make lasting professional connections.

learning as much as you can about math is helpful to create a solid base for future learning. These courses will prepare you for the more intensive coursework that is required to earn a bachelor's degree in computer science, information technology (IT), engineering, mathematics, or another field related to virtual, augmented, and mixed reality.

Additionally, many schools, libraries, and local organizations offer basic graphic design, animation, or audio design classes for free. These are another helpful option to look into. These courses can provide a foundation for future software development and coding courses.

Taking a psychology class might seem like a less obvious part of the preparation process. However, the material could be incredibly relevant and helpful because it directly relates to understanding people. This sort of human understanding is useful to developing user experiences. The information learned in these classes might also be helpful in developing strong interpersonal skills.

SKILLSETS FOR SUCCESS

Jobs in this field require many skills in addition to technical ones. For instance, as an engineer, it is important to know how to work both independently and on a team. Similarly, engineering jobs require strong problem-solving skills, attention to detail, and the ability to multitask.

Overall, for this line of work, it is important to develop soft skills. These are skills that you do not necessarily learn in a classroom. These skills include common sense, the ability to deal with people, and a positive, flexible attitude. These skills often grow out of experience and include things such as communication, adaptability, being observant, conflict resolution, and leadership.

Strong communication skills are some of the main factors to being successful in almost every career. Not only is it important to be able to express your ideas and thoughts clearly, but if something goes wrong or isn't working, it's important that you're able to let your team or supervisor know. Engineers must be able to communicate with each other and with other professionals in the field to design the best possible machines. Strong communication skills can lead to adaptability, which means being able to adjust when things don't go as planned. Engineers do this all the time when examining prototypes and determining what is and isn't benefiting the product or system as a whole.

Strong adaptability skills can develop from being observant. Being observant is similar to being curious. It means that you're aware of your surroundings and that you pay attention to your interests and what excites you. Being naturally curious is something that drives engineers to problem-solve. Problem-solving is important because it's a pathway to making systems more efficient and useful. Wanting to know why things are the way that they are and how they can be made better is something that serves engineers well. Because there are so many new uses of VR/AR specifically, engineers need to be willing to work through technical issues and respond to users' needs.

Finally, engineers working in the VR/AR field must be exceptional leaders. This is because engineers are at the forefront of this new and exciting field. It's up to them to decide what might be possible and how it can be achieved. They are responsible for doing things that have never been done before and must trust themselves and their teams to work together to create new programs and solutions.

HIGH SCHOOL RESOURCES

One of the best things that you can do at this stage of your education is to talk to your school guidance counselor. A guidance counselor is someone who is available to help you navigate college and personal decisions. They can help you further explore your interests. Once you get to high school, your guidance counselor will be a helpful point person for all of your college- and career-related questions. They will be able to inform you about programs your school offers or community connections that provide opportunities for students to gain access to software development training and other relevant experiences.

Another option to explore is vocational schools or technical programs. A vocational school is one in which students learn job-specific skills. Sometimes these schools or programs are housed on college campuses. They provide students with access to advanced labs and other resources. Some vocational schools offer students the option to prepare for and take certification exams.

High school guidance counselors are helpful resources for answering college- and career-related questions.

This means that when you graduate, you already have industry-standard qualifications and recognition of your educational achievements.

Some examples of these programs include IT, engineering and robotics, computer technology, and design and drafting technology. A design and drafting technology program might

Engineering camps and vocational or technical programs help students learn job-specific skills and provide access to advanced labs and other resources.

BEST BUY TEEN TECH CENTERS

By 2030, over 80 percent of jobs are predicted to require tech skills. Best Buy Teen Tech Centers are a new resource to help prepare teens for these types of jobs. Most of the centers are located in bigger cities, in states like California, Texas, and Illinois. However, Best Buy is looking to expand to smaller cities and suburbs in the coming years. At the centers, teens can develop critical skills by participating in hands-on activities. They participate in these activities under the supervision of trained professionals in the field. Adolescents are provided with the opportunity to explore their interests in areas

Best Buy Teen Tech Centers provide tech training and hands-on activities year-round.

like coding, robotics, 3D design, filmmaking, and music production through these centers.

Best Buy partners with an organization called the Clubhouse Network. This network connects members to a global community of over one hundred locations in twenty countries. It provides extracurricular learning environments for young people from underserved communities.

The Clubhouse Network offers multiple programs for teens, including the Clubhouse-to-College/Career program. It is a college- and career-readiness program. It helps teens to feel comfortable using technology. The program gives them the chance to get to know software and hardware that might be useful in a future career. This program also often takes students on field trips to see relevant technological facilities. Additionally, the program partners with businesses to offer job shadowing and internship opportunities, and it hosts workshops on résumé writing, interviewing skills, and education planning.

Local clubhouse memberships are entirely free. Depending on the location, the programs serve kids as young as ten to twelve years old through high school. If you're interested in getting involved, you can find a full list of locations and contact information on the Clubhouse Network's website.

Public libraries provide access to free courses, books, and computers that you can use to explore your interests and possible career paths.

focus on providing students with foundational computer-aided design (CAD) skills by teaching them how to draw sketches, draft prototypes, and operate state-of-the-art equipment and software.

INTERNSHIPS AND VOLUNTEERING

Internship opportunities at large companies are often competitive and require students to be available to commute to the companies' offices. This means that these sorts of internships are usually available in places like Seattle, New York, and Silicon Valley in California.

Although it's often these large tech companies that advertise internships, it never hurts to ask local businesses or smaller companies. These places are also resources. Ask them if they're open to letting you volunteer in some capacity. You could also look into shadowing a professional in the field. To do this, you could contact a local software development company and ask if they might be willing to let you come to their office for the day. You'd be surprised at how many opportunities are available to middle and high school students.

You might also reach out to a local website designer. Website design is a great place to start practicing basic computer programming skills. Even if the work you're doing isn't directly related to extended reality or engineering, making connections and learning as much as you can about related fields will serve you well as you approach college and beyond.

Another good idea is to look into volunteer opportunities. There might be a technology summer camp for kids or an opportunity to teach computer classes at a local elementary school. Doing these things can help you build your résumé, in addition to helping you develop those soft skills.

LOCAL AND ONLINE RESOURCES

Another great place to look to for resources is your local public library. Many public libraries provide access to free introductory-level courses. These courses are on topics like coding, software development, editing, 3D modeling, and design. Plus, you can request books and use the library's computers to access websites and articles that you find interesting. Taking an interest in your local community and the resources it has to offer can help you secure relevant internships and jobs later on.

If you live in a place that doesn't offer a wide range of resources, there are plenty of online courses as well. A wide range of these are free. Webites like Codeacademy.com teach students early HTML as well as JavaScript and Flash—used to add dimension and special features to a web page—using step-by-step instructions and videos.

MAKING CONNECTIONS TO VIRTUAL AND AUGMENTED REALITY

Whether you want to create video games, design military ships, or work with entrepreneurs to develop start-up ideas, it's important that you know how computers work. It's also important that you have a good understanding of how computers are used to make people's lives and jobs easier.

One of the best things you can do in middle school and high school is to follow your curiosity and ask lots of questions. Again, your high school guidance counselor should be able to connect you to local professionals who will most likely be more than happy to talk with you about their careers and any other questions that you might have.

5 FORECASTING THE FUTURE

Extended reality is still an emerging field. That means that the opportunities for careers in the field are growing and changing as the technology grows and changes itself. This provides an exciting opportunity for students to be at the forefront of development in this field. It also allows for the potential to discover and create new jobs.

WHERE IS VR/AR HEADED?

In a 2017 study, International Data Corp predicted a nearly 100 percent increase in spending on AR and VR technologies worldwide between 2017 and 2021. The study also predicted that United States consumers alone would spend $6.8 billion on AR and VR technology in 2018.

Opposite: The VR/AR job market is expected to expand in the coming years, providing exciting new opportunities for people looking to break into the field.

National Guard recruits use virtual reality combat simulators at training facilities, providing insight into the career path.

While it's great that there's a financial backing for the advancement of VR/AR, it's important that there is a workforce that's qualified to do the work being funded. Finding workers with the skill set required for VR/AR development is challenging because the industry is still so new.

EON Reality is a small virtual and augmented reality software developer headquartered in Irvine, California. It has partnered with several colleges around the country to offer training programs. These programs aim to bring students interested in the field up to speed on the skills necessary to be successful in a related career.

Lehman College in the Bronx, New York, is one of the schools EON Reality has partnered with. Its virtual reality training program lasts just eleven months and costs $1,300. Many consider this a small investment since most general engineers make between $60,000 and $80,000 each year. The coursework in these programs includes animation, coding, 3D graphic design, and web design.

While a natural curiosity and an interest in the field are important to the success of VR/AR engineering students, most of the technical skills can actually be taught on the job. This makes it so that no prior experience in web design or coding is necessary.

COMMERCIALIZATION AND EXPANSION

Large companies like Google, Samsung, Microsoft, IBM, and Apple are dominating the field in many ways right now. Even so, smaller start-up companies tend to offer high-quality software design and developer positions as well. They also provide lots of room to grow since the demand for jobs continues to increase.

While the gaming industry has given VR/AR the biggest boost in recent years, opportunities in architecture, engineering, construction, and many other fields continue to increase. According to a 2016 *Forbes* article, Indeed.com, a website used to list and find jobs, saw an 800 percent increase in VR/AR positions in just a two-year time span.

Many current jobs are focused on software development because companies want to commercialize the technology

Large companies like Google are leaders in the VR/AR field, but smaller start-up companies are also key players.

as quickly as possible. This means that they want to invest their resources in a way that brings in a profit, which they can do by increasing widespread usage and providing easier access. System developers, software developers, user experience designers, and graphic and visual artists are just a few examples of people who are helpful to companies hoping to expand their VR/AR applications.

MARKETING AND TECHNOLOGY

Engineering and software development jobs are the most obvious careers in the VR/AR field. However, there are many lesser known but equally important career paths to consider. A lot of these jobs are focused on soft skills that tend to be transferable across different industries. We imagine engineers using technology in their day-to-day

EYE TRACKING: THE TOBII VIRTUAL REALITY ANALYTICS TOOL

Tobii is a Swedish company that's a world leader in eye-tracking technology. This advanced technology is designed to be controlled by human eyes. This means that a device or computer is programmed to know when a user is looking at it, allowing people to visually interact with computers. An eye tracker is made up of cameras, projectors, and algorithms. Algorithms are sets of rules that computers are programmed to use to calculate or problem-solve. Patterns of light are projected onto a user's eyes. Then, the cameras create high-quality images of those patterns and the user's eyes. The algorithms use those images to calculate the positioning of the eyes. They can also determine where a person is looking on the screen. This allows users to select, zoom, point, and execute actions in more efficient and natural ways than can be done using a mouse or touchpad.

Tobii's goal with eye tracking is to humanize technology. This means technology can better understand users' intentions and goals. The information gathered through eye tracking can be used to create more intuitive, or instinctive, user experiences and computers. The technology can also provide information about a person's mental state. For example, it can evaluate how present or focused a person is during a task. It can also determine whether or not that person is drowsy.

Tobii has developed a VR tool that allows engineers to conduct eye-tracking studies within 3D virtual reality environments. The tool comes with features for measuring what a user sees. It also tracks their engagement with the simulated world. Heat maps, or graphic

Eye-tracking technology is programmed to know where a user is looking, which allows people to visually interact with a computer.

representations of data in which values are represented by colors, can show which parts of a VR landscape receive the most attention. This can be helpful for engineers to know when evaluating a design. VR environments like these that show the way people engage with virtually-created environments provide insight into how people navigate around a space. This is useful in helping engineers design better systems and environments.

For example, civil engineers can easily go back and forth between different versions of a building's layout and focus on where users had the most difficulty navigating. They can use that information to alter the design. In construction, they can determine the best placement of signs, such as emergency exits, by determining where users are most likely to look for them.

Communications professionals in marketing and sales work with engineers to understand the best ways to market products.

jobs and developers carefully creating that technology. However, how do the engineers decide which technology to rely on? How do the designers know how to make their products stand out? This is where marketing and sales come into play. Because so much of the focus over recent years has been on fine-tuning the technology and testing out various applications, these marketing and sales jobs are relatively new, but they are still very valuable.

So, if you're interested in the engineering side of virtual and augmented reality, it doesn't necessarily mean that you have to become an engineer. You can work alongside engineers to understand the best ways in which to market their products. You also may be able to get experience shadowing someone who markets the VR/AR technologies.

That said, don't hesitate to jump into the exciting STEM classes needed to become an engineer. There's no reason not to get started on this new and growing career path now.

GLOSSARY

algorithm A rule that computers are programmed to use to calculate or problem-solve.

applications (apps) Specialized programs designed and programmed to carry out a specific function.

augmented reality (AR) This type of computer programming adds digital, computer-generated elements to a user's existing field of vision; in this way, it augments, or adds to, a person's existing reality.

computer-aided engineering (CAE) This type of building and design is controlled or supported by computer systems used to draft and manufacture.

entrepreneur A person who starts and manages a business.

ethics The principles of right and wrong behavior.

experiential learning The process whereby knowledge is gained through direct participation in hands-on activities.

extended reality (XR) This term refers to all virtual and augmented realities and environments.

eye-tracking technology An advanced technology that follows a user's eye movements and knows when and where a user is looking, allowing someone to control a device with their eyes.

haptics The use of touch feedback to interact with a device.

HTML Short for "hypertext markup language," a computer programming language often used to design and develop web pages.

intrapreneur An organizational employee who is given freedom and support to create new products, services, or systems for the company.

mixed reality An emerging technology that combines both VR and AR to provide users with a fuller, more immersive experience.

optimize To design to perform in the most effective way.

prototype An initial model of a product or good that can be tested and recreated.

soft skills Qualities that allow for someone to interact well with others.

spectrum A scale or conceptual framework in which things or ideas are classified as falling between two extreme or opposite points.

STEM An acronym for the fields of science, technology, engineering, and mathematics.

virtual reality (VR) The use of computer graphics, sound, and other simulation technology to create a completely artificial environment that users can interact with.

vocational school A school in which people learn how to do a job that requires special skills.

FURTHER INFORMATION

Books

Allen, John. *Improving Virtual Reality*. Real-World Stem. San Diego: ReferencePoint Press, 2017.

Challoner, Jack. *Virtual Reality*. New York: DK Publishing, 2017.

Cooper, Nate. *Build Your Own Website: A Comic Guide to HTML, CSS, and WordPress*. San Francisco: No Starch Press, 2014.

Moritz, Jeremy. *Code for Teens: The Awesome Beginner's Guide to Programming*. Herndon, VA: Mascot Books, 2018.

Websites

Code.org

https://code.org

Code.org is a nonprofit organization dedicated to expanding students' access to computer science, providing leading K–12 curriculum.

Digital Responsibility

http://www.digitalresponsibility.org

Technology is part of our daily lives, but we have an obligation to use and share it responsibly. Digital Responsibility was started by a group of Silicon Valley tech employees to educate young people on the personal and public implications of technology.

Girls Who Code

https://girlswhocode.com/clubs

Girls Who Code offers free programs for girls in grades three to twelve. They develop coding and computer science skills to solve problems relevant to their communities.

Khan Academy

https://www.khanacademy.org

Khan Academy offers free practice exercises, instructional videos, and personalized learning to encourage and empower students interested in a variety of subjects, including computer science, math, and programming.

Videos

Computer Assisted Virtual Environment—CAVE

https://www.youtube.com/watch?v=M16mz8Pc_OM

The Idaho National Laboratory is one of the United States Department of Energy's laboratories. This video from the lab discusses how CAVE technology is a powerful research and education tool.

Pretty Curious—360° Virtual Reality— STEM Careers of the Future

https://www.youtube.com/watch?v=X3Dakpctg3o

EDF Energy is a company using virtual reality experiences to advance research, software, and structural engineering. Three women discuss their jobs and the future of STEM careers.

SELECTED BIBLIOGRAPHY

Bell, Lee. "Ford Shows Off Its 3D Cave Automatic Virtual Environment." *Inquirer*, May 20, 2013. https://www.theinquirer.net/inquirer/ feature/2268800/ford-shows-off-its-3d-cave-automatic-virtual-environment.

"Best Buy Teen Tech Centers." Best Buy Corporate News and Information. Accessed November 5, 2018. https://corporate.bestbuy.com/community-relations-overview/teen-tech-centers.

Brandon, Bray, Nick Schonning, and Matt Zeller. "What Is Mixed Reality?" Microsoft Docs, March 20, 2018. https://docs.microsoft.com/en-us/windows/mixed-reality/mixed-reality.

"CityViewAR." Human Interface Technology Laboratory New Zealand. Accessed November 05, 2018. https://www.hitlabnz.org/index.php/products/cityviewar.

"Exploring Software Engineering: A Comprehensive
Guide to Careers and Top Employers." Computer
Science Online. Accessed November 5, 2018.
https://www.computerscienceonline.org/software-
engineering.

Fernández, Rodrigo Pérez, Verónica Alonso, Luis
Sánchez, and Reidar Tronstad. "Virtual Reality
in a Shipbuilding Environment." *Advances
in Engineering Software* 81 (2015): 30–40.
doi:10.1016/j.advengsoft.2014.11.001.

Frigo, Mauricio A., Ethel C. C. Da Silva, and Gustavo
F. Barbosa. "Augmented Reality in Aerospace
Manufacturing: A Review." *Journal of Industrial
and Intelligent Information* 4, no. 2 (2016).
doi:10.18178/jiii.4.2.125-130.

"Information Processing Techniques Office." Defense
Advanced Research Projects Agency. Accessed
November 20, 2018. https://www.darpa.mil/about-
us/timeline/ipto.

Pannoni, Alexandra. "Vocational High School Programs an Option for Teens." *US News & World Report*, October 20, 2014. https://www.usnews.com/education/blogs/high-school-notes/2014/10/20/vocational-high-school-programs-an-option-for-teens.

Rogers, Kate. "The Virtual Reality Industry Can't Stop Growing - but Supply of Workers Is Limited." CNBC, December 8, 2017. https://www.cnbc.com/2017/12/08/virtual-reality-continues-to-grow--but-supply-of-workers-is-limited.html.

"A Selected History of DARPA Innovation." Defense Advanced Research Projects Agency. Accessed November 20, 2018. https://www.darpa.mil/Timeline/index.html.

Strauss, Karsten. "Virtual Reality Jobs Jump in the Job Market." *Forbes*, May 11, 2016. https://www.forbes.com/sites/karstenstrauss/2016/05/11/virtual-reality-jobs-jump-in-the-job-market/#7f4545fc7548.

"What Is Eye Tracking?" Tobii Tech. Accessed November 05, 2018. https://www.tobii.com/tech/technology/what-is-eye-tracking.

"What Is the Difference Between Interaction Design and UX Design?" Interaction Design Foundation, 2015. https://www.interaction-design.org/literature/article/what-is-the-difference-between-interaction-design-and-ux-design.

INDEX

Page numbers in **boldface** refer to images.

ABOUT THE AUTHOR

Sara Chuirazzi is a reader and writer living in New York by way of Ohio. She received a bachelor's degree from Bucknell University in psychology and English with a concentration in creative writing. She currently works for Viking and Penguin Books and is a mentor with Girls Write Now, a nonprofit organization serving at-risk girls from New York City public high schools.